Daily Dose

Stretching Faith Beyond Measure

By

Dr. Donavan L. Outten

You are annointed!!!

All Scripture quotations are taken from the Holy Bible, New King James Version®, copyright © 1982 by Thomas Nelson, Inc.

Cover design and Text Layout by: Designs by Rachelle Harris - www.designsbyrachelle.com

Format Assistance by: Cynthia D. Johnson – www.diverseskillscenter.com

ISBN: 978-1496188250

Printed in the United States of America

Dedication

This book is dedicated to every fighter who feels that they have lost a round in life, but had the audacity to get back up and fight again because they believe that they are in the will of God.

Acknowledgements

First and foremost, I would like to thank my Lord and Savior Jesus Christ who is the head of my life. Thank you for giving me the strength, the will and endurance to complete this book. Thank you for working through me to interpret Your Word so that it may touch the lives of others. Thank you for listening to my many prayers and the many blessings that you continued to give me throughout this process. Lord, I just want to say thank you for not giving up on me when I wanted to give up on myself. For that I say thank you.

I am eternally grateful to my family and friends who have supported me over the years; you are my foundation. Thank you for your continual support, confidence and your prayers.

Dr. Donavan L. Outten

Table of Contents

Introduction

Daily Dose is filled with declarations to help reinforce the Word of God as well as strengthen your spirit in man. These declarations should be repeated throughout the day to keep you focused on God's promises.

Life is filled with many uncertainties, and tomorrow is not promised. You have to make the most of everyday; especially this day. Do not hold grudges against your neighbor because that anger is only consuming you. Do not worry about situations that are out of your control because God is in control.

The Bible says in Romans 10:17, "So then faith cometh by hearing, and hearing by the word of God." In order to hear God's word, we must partake of it daily. Experiencing God's word comes in many forms: reading the Bible, regularly attending church services and Bible study classes, listening to your favorite Christian or Gospel CD, etc.

Regardless of the manner in which you intake the Word, it is best to get daily doses to stay armed against the attacks of the enemy. Just as we take all medications prescribed by healthcare providers, we need to take our spiritual medication as well.

In this collection of daily spiritual affirmations, Dr. Donavan Outten equips readers with daily "pick-me-ups" addressing areas of concern such as faith, blessings, revelation and destiny. Each "dose" is filled with a scripture-laced declaration that readers may avow throughout the day.

Daily Dose offers practical language that readers will feel comfortable reciting day or night to help guide them through any issue. This book allows readers to speak those things that are not as though they were, and call light into dark places. Watch the move of God in your life as you speak these positive affirmations and walk in the FOG – Favor of God!

Daily Dose's declarations are a constant reminder of what is important in your life. Be blessed, and remember to take daily doses of the Word of God!

Peace

I Will Look For Inner Peace

This is the day the LORD has made. Let us rejoice in it. Whenever an apparent challenge does appear, the revealing light of God directs me to look past the appearance of what I am experiencing with my senses. The illumination of Spirit is the source of my inner light. I turn towards that inner voice and listen to what God has to say to me, and I know He will always keep and protect me. "I will turn the darkness before them into light, the rough places into level ground. These are the things I will do, and I will not forsake them." Isaiah 42:16

Today's Declaration:

Although today I face trials and tribulations on every side, God is with me. His grace is sufficient for me and His power is made perfect in weakness.
2 Corinthians 12:9

Courage under Fire

There are times when your heart breaks and you must do what you don't want to do to get ahead. Swallow your pride and humble yourself and know that those tears are temporary. Joy and peace are coming. Psalm 126:5 "Those who sow in tears will reap with songs of joy." A winner never stays down for long. You need to have that 'Get Up' spirit.

Today's Declaration:

I push forward in the name of the LORD. I go to everyone He sends me and I say whatever He commands me. I am not afraid of their faces for God is with me and will rescue me. I have an important assignment within the Kingdom of God that I must complete. Jeremiah 1:7-8

Seek God's Peace for Your Life

I charge you to go out into the deepness of your soul and seek the soul saving revelations in your life. Make changes in your life in ways that only you could prosper and receive inner peace. In the book of Job, when he was at his last and all was taken away, he continued to trust God. Look at his miraculous end! Don't be 'ye of little faith!' All it takes is a mustard seed of faith to help your roots expand and branch out. You have the ability to look at your future while living in the present. This is a gift from God.

Today's Declaration:

I will forever learn. I have a teachable spirit and operate as an apostle, prophet, evangelist, pastor and teacher to prepare God's people for works of service so that the body of Christ may be built up. Ephesians 4:11-12

I Claim Peace in My Life

You should fear neither man nor any obstacle that confronts you. God is your shield and your everlasting light. Leviticus 26:6 "I will grant peace in the land, and you will lie down and no one will make you afraid. I will remove savage beasts from the land, and the sword will not pass through your country."

Today's Declaration:

I bless the LORD! He causes me to lie down and sleep in peace. He alone makes me dwell in safety. Psalm 4:8

May Peace Be In Your Life

What a Mighty God we serve! Blessings! May this morning fill you with love, joy, peace, light and PROSPERITY! God is in the building business, and He has a role for you. Money is just one benefit of what's to come. God is working a mold out of your life and is about to create some upset in hell. All those that thought you had it going on are in for a treat. Relax, be blessed and thank Him now for what is about to take place in your life. Shout, scream, praise, do whatever you feel the need to do, then face your opposition, and put your foot on its neck because it can no longer bind you. YOU BIND ALL THE SATANIC ATTACKS. Let peace be instilled in you today.

Today's Declaration:

Today, I am more than a conqueror. Hell can't stop this release that's about to manifest in my life. Though a mighty army surrounds me, my heart will not be afraid. Even if I am attacked, I will remain confident. Psalm 27:3

Strongholds Break Free

So many nights I worry about finances, my family, my health, and my future. But as I cry out to you, LORD, in prayer and ask for your mercy and grace, you assure me that joy cometh in the morning light. Psalm 30:5: "For his anger lasts only a moment, but his favor lasts a lifetime; weeping may remain for a night, but rejoicing comes in the morning."

Today's Declaration:

I look for God in all things. He is a refuge for the oppressed, a stronghold in times of trouble.
Psalm 9:9

Because Of God's Grace

The very thought of the goodness of the LORD causes my cup to run over with Joy. I am at peace with the world and myself. I am upheld by His grace. Psalm 3:5: "I lie down and sleep; I wake again, because the LORD sustains me."

Today's Declaration:

I praise the LORD with all my heart; I tell of all His wonders. I am glad and rejoice in God. I sing praises to your name, Most High God!
Psalm 9:1-2

Experience God's Peace

Just wanted to take a brief moment to share with you that you have once again made it by the Grace of God. With the wonderful Word of Jesus, I pray that you have a happy day and that the remainder of your week be filled with prosperity and the holy light. May it shine upon your footsteps that you may continue to walk in the path of greater blessings. A message from Philippians 4:6: "Don't worry about anything; instead pray about everything. Tell God what you need and thank Him for all He has done. If you do this, you will experience God's peace, which is far more wonderful than the human mind can understand." His peace will guard your heart and mind as you live in Christ Jesus.

Today's Declaration:

God's Word is forever guiding me. I keep God's Word in my heart. His Word is a lamp to my feet and a light to my path. Psalm 119:105

Allow Peace in Your House

Bare in mind, you have survived this week and are standing at the week's end. Praise God from whom all blessings flow. Again, you have defeated all obstacles and you are still alive. (Now, that's worth shouting about!) May God fully bless you and cleanse you this day. Obstacles should never stop you. Labor should never stagger you. Envy should never move you. Silly and petty gossip should never deter you. Pride should never overtake you. Hate should never rob you. Humility should be instilled within you. Put on your armor and stand firmly. Put the devil in his place.

Today's Declaration:

This is the day I overcome! I am strong in the LORD and in the power of His might. I put on the whole armor of God, withstanding in the evil day. After I have done all, I stand. I am more than a conqueror! Ephesians 6:10, 13

Obedience

My Faith Sustains Me

Faith assures me that with God all things are possible. And with faith, I can do all things. 2 Chronicles 20:20: "Early in the morning they left for the Desert of Tekoa. As they set out, Jehoshaphat stood and said, 'Listen to me, Judah and people of Jerusalem! Have faith in the LORD your God and you will be upheld; have faith in his prophets and you will be successful.'" You will always be successful as long as you have faith in the Almighty!

Today's Declaration:

I stand firmly on the Word of God! I do not fear the threats of man. I am from God and have overcome them. The one who is in me is greater than the one in the world. Who would dare come against God Almighty? 1 John 4:4

Let Go And Let God

Remember if you are going through the storm..."you may not be able to stop the storm from raging, but you can move away from the storm." Make a position move in your life. This is your season to advance, be stress-free, prosperous, happy, fulfilled. Don't hold on to situations (or people) that no longer fulfill you or bring you joy. If it's a job, use it long enough, but search diligently and aggressively for a role that you were created to perform. If it's a relationship that has lost meaning and causes more pain to hold on to, remember, you can't go back and change yesterday. Mark 7:8: "You have let go of the commands of God and are holding on to the traditions of men." Focus on what God has for you, not man, and you will always do the right thing.

Today's Declaration:

I will no longer waste time. The good life is awaiting my arrival. I've considered the ways of the ant. I am wise, storing provision in the summer and gathering food at harvest. Proverbs 6:6-8

Release Your Strongholds

Anything that has bound you, bothered you, or tried to hold you back, it or they won't prosper. It's time for you to put on your boxing gloves and get ready for this battle going on. The enemy is after your family, friends and you. It's time for you to fight back and claim what God has given you. Remove those ropes, chains and shackles and release that stronghold. This is your day, so claim it and let there be peace in it!

Today's Declaration:

I take back what's rightfully mine! I will no longer allow the enemy to defeat me. I will not ponder the negative circumstances. I will walk in peace. For this battle is not mine, but God's.
2 Chronicles 20:15

I Will Wait On What God Has For Me

Colossians 1:11 says, "...being strengthened with all power according to his glorious might so that you may have great endurance and patience, and joy." Revelation 14:12 says, "This calls for patient endurance on the part of the saints who obey God's commandments and remain faithful to Jesus." Know that you are enduring a season of patience and what God has for you is for you. There might be a good reason why you did not get that house or that job. Maybe it was God who protected you from it. Be of great endurance (long suffering) and patience. God will bless you not only with the house or job you deserve but also with your DREAM home or career. Don't worry; your blessing is coming. Remain in a spirit of expectancy!!

Today's Declaration:

I expect great things to happen in my life today! I receive great rewards from God. I am like a tree planted by the rivers of water that bring forth my fruit in my season. My leaves do not wither and whatever I do prospers. It is my time! Psalm 1:3

The Right People

God determines who walks into your life. It's up to you to decide who to let walk away and who to let stay. People come into your life for a reason, a season, and a lifetime. God allows this to happen so that we may grow and learn from other people. Don't keep those people in your life that were only supposed to be there for a season. Let them go. Grasp the wisdom of those that were sent for a reason. And embrace those who were sent for a lifetime.

Today's Declaration:

I surround myself with the right people. I realize that I am a chosen people, a royal priesthood, a holy nation, a people belonging to God. I declare the praises of Him who called me out of darkness into His wonderful light. 1 Peter 2:9

I Will Remain Faithful

Just take a minute to declare blessings for your friends, family and loved ones. Satan is always near and things can get testy at times. But throughout life, we have our battles and storms. I wish you joy first and then strength that you may be stronger than the battles you will fight. God said ye shall receive. God has plans and blessings waiting on you to claim. Try God and see His power work in your life. All you have to do is remain faithful to His word and believe in Him.

Today's Declaration:

Today, I am full of joy. I declare that I have life and have it more abundantly. There is nothing that can stop the plans God has for my life. John 10:10

Stand Strong and Don't Be Weary

The LORD has filled me with a message to share with you. No matter what happens today, bear in mind, "That no weapon formed against you shall prosper!" God is in the blessing business, and no matter what Satan throws your way it can't stop you. You control your destiny! Satan has many against you, but God is your army! Stand strong and be filled with faith and the Holy Spirit. God is your armor on the battlefield.

Today's Declaration:

I will not ponder the negative circumstances. I will walk in peace. For this battle is not mine, but God's. 2 Chronicles 20:15

Acknowledge the Lord in All Ways

I hope that you are able to attain the goals that you have set for yourself today and for weeks to come. Don't force it; just let it happen naturally. Sometimes when we try to "make" things happen, we fail to see that they are already happening and much to our favor.   Jesus said to the father, "You said, all things are possible for the one who believes! Help me to believe more." Have a wonderful day and continue to walk in the direction that your steps have been ordered to. Peace and blessings. Trust in the LORD with all thy heart; and lean not unto thy own understanding. In all thy ways acknowledge him, and he shall direct thy paths. -Proverbs 3:5-6

Today's Declaration:

I don't trust in man, but my confidence is in God. I trust in the LORD with all my heart and not my own understanding.   I acknowledge Him in all my ways. He directs my paths. Psalm 3:5-6

Because God Said So

You never want to give something greater to someone who is less deserving because God himself deemed that you have it. The LORD is looking for genuine people who he can appoint to lead his people, and with greatness comes great responsibility. 1 Samuel 13:14: "But now your kingdom will not endure; the LORD has sought out a man after his own heart and appointed him leader of his people, because you have not kept the LORD's command." If you don't do what the LORD asks you to do, you will never have what you are supposed to have.

Today's Declaration:

I praise God Almighty! He has blessed me with many skills and abilities. I will use what He has given me to advance His kingdom. Much is given to me, therefore much is required of me.
Luke 12:48

Walk in the Path
God Has For You

I woke up with a revelation and had to share it.
For all obstacles that have been placed before you,
today is the day. Take those obstacles, whether its
abuse, hard feelings, mistreatment, confusion and
use them to your advantage. This is the day God
wants us to use all the negative resources and
make blessings happen. I know you think it
sounds crazy, but the best way to defeat the devil
and opposition at its game is to use what is coming
at you and reverse it for good. There is no such
thing as bad. Bad is how we feel, and we can alter
that feeling by seeing the good in the bad. I wish
you patience and endurance on this journey. IT
WON'T BE EASY but the results will be well
worth the fight. God is on your side.

Today's Declaration:

*It's not over...reverse! God has called me blessed.
He has blessed me and no one can reverse it!
Numbers 23:19*

I Will Obey the Lord

The LORD is my salvation and my rock; there is no other like him. He is my foundation, and I will not let any strongholds bind me because my faith tells me that the LORD guides my path. Psalm 31:3: "For thou art my rock and my fortress; therefore for thy name's sake lead me, and guide me." Today, I refuse to walk in fear. I will no longer worry about yesterday...or tomorrow. I focus on today. Today is the day that the LORD has made. I will rejoice and be made glad in it! Lead me, dear LORD; I will follow you wholeheartedly.

Today's Declaration:

No matter what I face today, I am strong and very courageous. I am not terrified or discouraged. For the LORD my God is with me wherever I go. Joshua 1:9

Do Not Let Fear Overtake You

You need to have the faith of Daniel in the lion's den and not be afraid of any situation because the LORD our God is with you at all times. Deuteronomy 31:6: "Be strong and courageous. Do not be afraid or terrified because of them, for the LORD your God goes with you; he will never leave you nor forsake you." The LORD promises to keep you and protect you. He will never give you more than you can bear.

Today's Declaration:

God is able! He is strong and mighty. I am the head and not the tail; above only and never beneath because I keep the commands of the LORD and follow them carefully. Deuteronomy 28:13

I Will Survive the Storm

Exodus 15:2: "The LORD is my strength and my song; He has become my salvation. He is my God, and I will praise Him, my father's God, and I will exalt Him." If you truly believe this, you will conquer every obstacle, leap every hurdle, climb every mountain and defeat every enemy that will form against you. Know that God is your foundation, your rock and your strength!

Today's Declaration:

I am anointed of God and He loves me. He goes before me and levels the mountains. Nothing is too hard for God. Isaiah 45:2

Blessings

God Will Work Wonders

Blessings! No matter what time of day it is, God is on the move and He is working for the greater end for us. I wish you a blessing too big for you to receive. I pray God strengthens your heart and soul. All that are lost and strayed, I pray you find Him and reach out to Him no matter what the problem. Remember, all we need is the Master's touch. He healed a man with leprosy, a woman with an issue of blood and helped a blind man see. All it takes is a touch from Him. How badly do you want this deliverance? Don't wait by the pool for thirty-eight years waiting on 'someone' to help you. Help is here. All we must do is ask. Don't worry about 'how' He'll do it. God solved some serious issues in some crazy ways! (He restored a blind man's sight with mud made from His saliva and commanded him to wash in the Pool of Siloam. Sarah had a baby at the age of 90). Who can comprehend His ways? Overlook the 'how' and give a glorious praise to 'Who'-God Almighty! May God fill you with love and many blessings.

Today's Declaration:

Today, I won't try to figure out God. I won't live in doubt. I've made my requests in prayer. I believe that I have received them. Therefore I have them. To God be the glory! Mark 11:24-25

Greater Is Yours

There are miracles happening every day: cancers being healed, surviving car accidents, and job promotions. The LORD said 'if you believe in me I would do wonders for you.' Exodus 34:10: "Then the LORD said, 'I am making a covenant with you. Before all your people I will do wonders never before done in any nation in all the world. The people you live among will see how awesome is the work that I, the LORD, will do for you.'" Don't worry about what others have because your blessing is on the way.

Today's Declaration:

I trust in the LORD and His word. The grass withers and the flowers fall, but the word of God stands forever. Isaiah 40:8

There Is No Other Like Me

I am beautiful in design. This is the way God has made me. I am a king or queen in my own birthright, so I am royalty. There is no other like me in the world, so I am perfect in my own right with room to grow. I am destined for greatness and great shall I be.

Today's Declaration:

I am blessed of God and made in His likeness and image. I am fruitful and multiply. I subdue and have dominion over the earth. Genesis 1:26

Give Freely and Unconditionally

You are always such a blessing to others. The Bible says in Genesis 12:2: "I will make you into a great nation and I will bless you; I will make your name great, and you will be a blessing." You have been such a great blessing, and the LORD our God will make your name great. He will bless those that bless you. He will also give you favor because you are obedient and continue to do His will. Obedience is better than sacrifice. Today, meditate on your kingdom assignment and allow God to reveal His strategy to you. Are you prepared? Overflow is coming!

Today's Declaration:

God trusts me. God has given me dominion over the works of His hands and put all things under my feet. How majestic is His name in all the earth!
Psalm 8:6-9

May You Have a Generational Blessing

This is the day the LORD has made; let us rejoice in it. Deuteronomy 12:7 says, "There, in the presence of the LORD your God, you and your families shall eat and shall rejoice in everything you have put your hands to, because the LORD your God has blessed you." Yes, the LORD our God is in the blessing business and he has been blessing you. Have you recognized his blessings today? Take time out of your day and feel the power of God, and recognize His strength. He has blessed you and your family today, your situation today, your thoughts today, and your troubles will pass. God loves you and will always keep you.

Today's Declaration:

I am living a blessed life. I am blessed in the city and blessed in the country. Blessed is the fruit of my body. I am blessed coming in and going out. God has blessed me tremendously.
Deuteronomy 28:3-6

Be In The Presence Of God

When you are in the presence of God and doing His will, not only will you prosper but your children will prosper also. Your family is an extension of you. When you do good deeds, your blessings become your descendant's blessings as well. Psalm 25:13: He will spend his days in prosperity, and his descendants will inherit the land.

Today's Declarations:

I honor God by obeying His word. I train my children in the way they should go. And when they are old, they should not turn from it. My generations shall always praise and honor God. Proverbs 22:6

Favor Is Yours

Leviticus 26:9: "I will look on you with favor and make you fruitful and increase your numbers, and I will keep my covenant with you." God is about to open the heavens with blessings for you. All you have to do is continue to be His servant. Remember you have the favor of God and He wants you to succeed. God Almighty did not put you here to live off of bread and water alone. But your strength...and your success shall come from every word that proceeds from the mouth of God. Listen. What is He saying to you today?

Today's Declaration:

God has set before me life and death, blessings and curses. I choose life and blessings so that me and my children may live, love the LORD, listen to His voice and hold fast to Him.
Deuteronomy 30:19-20

Blessings Come
When You Least Expect It

When there is nothing left but God that is when you find out that God is all you need. People will come and go throughout your lifetime. You will have good days and bad days. But throughout it all, there is only one consistent factor, and that is God. He will never leave you nor forsake you. Deuteronomy 7:13: "He will love you and bless you and increase your numbers. He will bless the fruit of your womb, the crops of your land—your grain, new wine and oil."

Today's Declaration:

This day, I declare that I am strong and courageous. I am not afraid or terrified; for God goes with me. He will never leave me or forsake me. Deuteronomy 3:6

If You Obey

Obey God's commandments and you shall reap the rewards that He has promised you. Order my steps in your word, dear LORD. Lead and guide me all of my days. Deuteronomy 5:33: "Walk in all the ways that the LORD your God has commanded you, so that you may live and prosper and prolong your days in the land that you will possess." The LORD said that man should not live off of bread and water alone, but by every word that proceeds from the mouth of God.

Today's Declaration:

I'm living the abundant life, reaping the promises God made to me. The Word and commands of God are in my mouth and on my heart. I will obey the Word and commands of God. Deuteronomy 30:14

Enlarge My Territory

Just wanted to send you blessings on God's Day and I hope that your blessings last all week long. God is in the blessing business, and you are in line for a break through. If you do nothing more, ask God to bless you indeed and enlarge your territory. I won't tell you the results, but if you recite it daily, you will see. Your faith will make it happen!

Today's Declaration:

Thank you, LORD for hearing my prayer! Thank you for blessing me and enlarging my territory. Thank you that your hand is with me. Thank you for keeping me from harm. Thank you, LORD, for granting me my requests! 2 Chronicles 4:10

God Is a Healer

God Can Do the Impossible

I just wanted to share with you the prayer of David and wish you peace as you enter into this week. Psalms 86:1-7: "Bend down, O LORD, and hear my prayer; answer me, for I need your help. Protect me, for I am devoted to you. Save me, for I serve you and trust you. Be merciful, O LORD for I am calling out to you constantly. Give me happiness, O LORD, for my life depends on you. Oh LORD, you are so good, so ready to forgive, so full of unfailing love for all who ask your aid. Listen closely to my prayer, O LORD, hear my urgent cry. I will call you whenever trouble strikes and you will answer me." In reading this prayer, may He fill you with all your needs. There is nothing too hard for God. Nothing! No matter what your situation, condition or position, absolutely nothing is too difficult for God. Go ahead...trust in Him. Dare to surrender, exhale, relax and enjoy the ride!

Today's Declaration:

I lean on and trust in God today. He is the bread of life. I come to Him so I will never go hungry. I believe in Him and I will never be thirsty. Streams of living water flow within me.
John 6:35-36, John 7:38

In The Name Of Jesus

The presence of God is the one power in my life, a healing presence that gives me energy and strength and a renewed sense of oneness with the Creator. Do I need to be healed? I take a moment to become still and feel God's healing power. The life of God is a real presence in every cell of my body, a presence that restores health and sparks renewal wherever it is needed. "Heal me, O LORD, and I shall be healed; save me, and I shall be saved." -- Jeremiah 17:14

Today's Declaration:

I am healed! My light breaks forth like the dawn and my healing quickly appears. My righteousness goes before me and the glory of the LORD is my rear guard. Isaiah 58:8

Yesterday Is Gone and Today Is Here

In Philippians 1:6 it says, "I started a good work in you and what I start I shall finish." No matter how you see your life, He is still working on you and your best is yet to come. Without the struggle, there is no gain. But as we all know, in order to see the rainbow, you must stand a little rain. May God fill you with light to shine the way, peace to clear your mind, joy and love that you may be a blessing to someone. Remember the only thing that can hurt you is worrying, fear, and stress. Why worry? What's going to be will be. Why stress? What's done is in the past. Why fear? It's not from God. Know that God will hold you and never forsake you. It is written.

Today's Declaration:

I am finally living life; life is no longer living me! I have forgotten the former things. I don't dwell on the past. God is doing a new thing in my life. Isaiah 43:18

Renew My Spirit

There are times we consider the enemy to be operating against our lives, when in fact, the enemy is within us. We can be our worst enemy. We are quick to judge others, to complain...but we never look at ourselves. Today, take a look within. What do you see? Are you satisfied with what you see? Most importantly, is God pleased with what is within you?

Today's Declaration:

Today, I will look within myself and consider my own ways. LORD, create in me a clean heart and renew a steadfast spirit within me. Psalm 51:10

Send Me a New Anointing

God is healing and renewing you right now. You have to ask God to send you a new anointing so you can receive your new blessings today. God will continue to anoint you throughout your life but you must ask Him to do so. Exodus 40:9: "Take the anointing oil and anoint the tabernacle and everything in it; consecrate it and all its furnishings, and it will be holy." In order for you to be holy you must ask and receive your new anointing.

Today's Declaration:

LORD, anoint me this day. I am holy because my Father is holy. I prepare my mind for action. I am self-controlled and set my hope fully on the grace to be given me when Jesus Christ is revealed. 1 Peter 1:13

You Will Never Handle More Than You Can Bear

When you have those days that are stormy and the path seems to be rough, just know that you are a prayer away from your next breakthrough. The LORD has a way of restoring your faith and commitment to any situation. Psalm 23:3: "He restoreth my soul: He leadeth me in the paths of righteousness for his name's sake." The LORD will restore, replenish, refill, and rejuvenate your mind body and soul when you need it.

Today's Declaration:

The glory of the Lord is upon me. Your hands made me and formed me; give me understanding to learn your commands. May those who fear you rejoice when they see me, for I have put my hope in your word. Psalm 119:73-74

Lord Heal My Soul

The healing power of God is within me. He does His perfect work, and I will continuously be made whole again. The LORD our God is healing our very soul. Every failure and wicked thing that has been cast upon us shall not prevail. But the Spirit of the living God shall dwell within me and I shall prosper.

Today's Declaration:

I am healed. I declare that I prosper in all things and be in good health, just as my soul prospers! 3 John 2

No More Pain

LORD I am thanking you because I made it through the stormy days. I am thanking you because you gave me strength to jump over hurdles and walk around obstacles. I am thanking you because you protect me from hurt, harm and danger-seen and unseen. 1 Chronicles 16:34: "Give thanks to the LORD, for he is good; his love endures forever." LORD I am thanking you for all that I am and all that I have.

Today's Declaration:

God sustains me. God loves me. He keeps my steps from stumbling. When I lie down, I am not afraid. He causes my sleep to be sweet.
Proverbs 4:23-24

Never a Problem He Can't Solve

Whatever your problems are today, let them go and give them to God. He will handle every situation and circumstance that has and will come your way. Psalm 55:22: "Cast your cares on the LORD and he will sustain you; he will never let the righteous fall." You will never be lost if Jesus is by your side. Think about it...has there ever been a problem He couldn't solve? An issue He didn't know about? A tear He never saw? Or a heartache He never felt? No...He's always been there and He's there now! He loves you tremendously!

Today's Declaration:

I look beyond my circumstances. I am excited about what God is doing in my life! He made plans for me; plans to prosper me and not to harm me; plans to give me hope and a future.
Jeremiah 29:11

God Is a Deliverer

No Matter the Situation

What kind of day would it be without God? I will leave that open. God is still on the move. I won't bombard you with all to come, for some like surprises. God has something for you and it's big. No matter what the day seems like, you will survive. Stop thinking about the pressures and challenges of the days that have past. Today marks the beginning of greater things for you. John 14 states: "LET NOT YOUR HEART BE TROUBLED." Enjoy today and live each day as if it were your last. May you be filled with love and light and peace, but most of all, WITH GOD!

Today's Declaration:

My past mistakes and misfortunes no longer haunt me. I do not fear disgrace and will not be humiliated. God has caused me to forget the shame of my youth. I have decided to live life to the fullest! Isaiah 54:4

Victory Is Mine

What kind a day would it be without me thanking God for such good friends and family? I wish them love and happiness! If you are enjoying the praise and accepting what God is planning to do in your life, you should be feeling a wonderful sensation. God is moving and making a way for you. You may not see the blessing right away, but you should feel the mountain of struggle lifting from you. Awake, be patient, and be of good cheer; God is on the way. When you are able to pray for others before you pray for yourself God will certainly bless you!

Today's Declaration:

I receive the Word of the LORD. He has declared that He will set me in praise, fame and honor high above all the nations He has made. I am a people holy to the LORD, as He promised.
Deuteronomy 26:19

Your Blessing Is About To Come

I pray God be with you and strengthen you as you continue to make it through this week. If you have had any trials, know that you must first go through the fire and stay prayerful because the best is yet to come. Or as saints say, 'God is on His way and bringing an abundant blessing for you.' If all has been well, know that it's God's way of showing you He is here and that's just a taste of what's to come. Are you ready to fully receive the blessings and favor of the LORD? Yes! The best is yet to come!

Today's Declaration:

The best is yet to come! I am walking in the favor of the LORD. He has granted me abundant prosperity. I shall receive all that God has for me while in the land of the living.
Deuteronomy 28:11

Out of a Bad Situation

Once again, God is in the blessing business! No matter what last night may have brought or the struggles of today, you have once again made it. You have survived all that tried to take you down. You have reached another great victory. Instead of sending a prayer, I am charging you to try God. Ask for something so great...I promise when you least expect it, your blessing will appear. May He lay to rest all of this week's dilemmas that you may start next week off fresh. God bless you and know that 'No weapon formed against you or your family shall prosper.'

Today's Declaration:

No one or nothing can hinder the plans God has for my life. No weapon formed against me will prosper and I condemn every tongue that accuses me. Isaiah 54:17

Put Your Trust in God

Trust in the LORD with all your heart; do not depend on your own understanding. Seek His will in all you do and He will direct your path. Today, I charge you to do this and watch the blessings flow. I wish you joy and happiness. When life does not make sense, I wish you understanding. Continue to be mindful of what God has in store for you. Be still and let God do His mighty work to bless you. Today, resist putting your hands in God's work. Let Him handle it for you.

Today's Declaration:

Great is the LORD God Almighty! Nothing is too difficult for Him. I declare God is my strong tower! He bestows glory on me and lifts up my head. Psalm 3:3

God Is My Source

Looking beyond current circumstances, I perceive my life with clarity. I see past seeming obstacles to the potential that lies within each new day. Christ in me, He is my source of unlimited potential. I am moving forward in accepting and fulfilling my divine potential day by day. "The kingdom of God is not coming with things that can be observed; nor will they say, 'Look, here it is!' or 'There it is!' For, in fact, the kingdom of God is among you."--Luke 17:20-21

Today's Declaration:

My assignment in the Kingdom of God is vital. I keep my eyes on God. I have been placed in a position of royalty for such a time as this. I will accomplish the task. Esther 4:14

It Will Come To Pass

Let's get driven, be persistent, and thrive for excellence! Don't let anyone tell you that you can't do it, especially if God was the one who ordained it for you. 2 Kings 19:25: "Have you not heard? Long ago I ordained it. In days of old I planned it; now I have brought it to pass." Don't sleep on God's mission! Awake and arise to your true calling. Destiny awaits....

Today's Declaration:

I am committed to complete the task God has assigned me. Here I am, LORD, send me! I'll go and tell the people! Isaiah 6:8-9

Your Breakthrough Is Coming

Your heart has many desires, needs and wants. The LORD knows them all because He created you. Whether your heart desires a new house, a better job or a successful and happy relationship, you have to take it to God. Ask and it shall be given to you. The LORD did not put you here to live off of bread and water alone. Open your heart and let the guidance of the Spirit continually open a new world of possibilities to you. "Ask, and it will be given you; search, and you will find; knock, and the door will be opened for you."--Matthew 7:7. How strong is your faith? Try God today and ask for all that you need, want and desire and have the faith that He will grant you everything. Dare to elevate your current level of belief.

Today's Declaration:

Nothing can keep me off track. I am a faithful servant of the Most High God. Love and faithfulness remain with me. I have won favor and a good name with God and man. Psalm 3:3-4

God Can Do All Things

God is in the moving and making over business! If you think it's time to move forward whether it be with work, relationships, your spiritual connections, that project you have been wanting to do, or whatever it is, now is the time. God is ready to work with you and see you succeed. If you have taken the wrong road only to find a dead end, stop. Before you take another step, consult God within you. Express your deepest desires and fears. Tell Him, 'I've been on this journey and I need you to make me over so while I walk the right road you will guide me.' God can do things we never imagined and now it is your time. Trust God and believe that nothing can stop you from the greatness but yourself.

Today's Declaration:

I am truly blessed. God has opened doors for me. No one can shut them, not even me. He prepares a table before me in the presence of my enemies. He anoints my head with oil; my cup overflows. Psalm 23:5

Erase All Negativity
Out of My Life

The everlasting joy of the Holy Spirit within me eradicates all belief in depression, despair, dejection and sorrow. I am filled with unspeakable joy today. Deuteronomy 16:15: "For seven days celebrate the Feast to the LORD your God at the place the LORD will choose. For the LORD your God will bless you in all your harvest and in all the work of your hands, and your joy will be complete."

Today's Declaration:

I seek God with all my heart today. The light of God's face shines on me, for He has filled my heart with greater joy. Psalm 4:6-7

It's On the Way

I am inspired to share with you a scripture from Philippians 4:19 that states, "God will supply all your needs!" This is so important to know. You are not alone and need not worry; God will supply your needs. I pray that He fills all your needs, wants, and desires. I know that you will receive an abundance of joy and peace and that your week will be filled with pleasurable things. God wants you to live more abundantly and He has blessings to help you along the way! Be patient…its coming!

Today's Declaration:

I will not waste time worrying. God has chosen me and not rejected me. I do not fear, for He is with me. I am not dismayed. God strengthens and helps me. He upholds me with His righteous right hand. Isaiah 41:9-10

Love

Rejoice in God's love

Live in the presence of the divine light that illuminates the way to God. Live for today and live in the moment. Know that you can cast your cares on Him and all will be fine. God will guide you through your darkest moments, and He will rejoice with you in your most precious and joyful moments as well.

Today's Declaration:

I have a personal relationship with God. He loves me. Before He formed me in the womb, He knew me. He chose me. Before I was born He set me apart and appointed me as a prophet to the nations. Jeremiah 1:5

Love the Lord with Thy Heart

I make a total self-commitment to God and praise Him daily. I honor and respect the LORD my God with an open heart, mind and soul. Exodus 15:2 The LORD is my strength and my song; he has become my salvation. He is my God, and I will praise Him, my father's God, and I will exalt Him. The more you praise God, the more you will receive your blessings.

Today's Declaration:

I worship the LORD with all that I am. Holy, holy, holy is the LORD Almighty! The whole earth is full of His glory. Isaiah 6:3

God's Love Is Free

God so loved the world that he gave His only begotten son that we may live free of sin and be offered eternal life. I charge you to see that if God risked His own for you, then just imagine what else He will do for you. God has blessings falling faster than you know and one of those many blessings has your name on it. Know that God wants you to be filled with love, light, laughter, and peace. He wants you to succeed and prosper and do His will.

Today's Declaration:

Today is my best day yet. God has sent a blessing on my house and everything I put my hands to prospers. He has already blessed me in the land He is giving me. Deuteronomy 28:8

Love Others like You Love God

I just wanted to take a minute and wish you blessings. May God fill you with Love, Peace and Good Fortune. Our workload sometimes consumes us, but by the grace of God we always pull through. Say a prayer for a loved one today. Don't make this day about you, but make it about someone else's blessing. Pray that your prayer reaches that person in perfect health and spirit. Always keep God First!

Today's Declaration:

I am strong and my bloodline is strong. There are non-feeble among us. Unwholesome talk does not escape our mouths, but only what is helpful for building others up according to their needs, that it may benefit those who listen.
Ephesians 4:29

A Praying Family

The family that prays together stays together. The devil is not just after you but he is after your family. Your entire family needs to be covered by the blood of Jesus. Deuteronomy 7:9: "Know therefore that the LORD your God is God; he is the faithful God, keeping his covenant of love to a thousand generations of those who love him and keep his commands". Pray together for years to come and make it a family tradition so that the next generation will know Christ as LORD.

Today's Declaration:

We are a praying family. God has set before me life and death, blessings and curses. I choose life and blessings so that I and my children may live, love the LORD, listen to His voice and hold fast to Him. Deuteronomy 30:19-20

In God's Image

Have you ever just thought about how amazing God is? Don't concentrate on the material things He's provided. But look deeper than that. Look at how He formed you. He's so amazing that He created us all without duplication, but yet, He created us in His likeness and image. He desires us to be His duplicates on the earth. Think about that! God's duplicate! An ambassador of Christ! Pure royalty! It's no wonder we are fearfully and wonderfully made! Who could deny a God like this?

Today's Declaration:

God knows me and loves me deeply. He is mindful of me and cares for me. He made me lower than the heavenly being and crowned me with glory and honor. Psalm 8:4-5

God's Love Is Powerful

The very definition of love is God because God is love. God wants you to love thy neighbor, love thy family and love thy self as you would love Him. Deuteronomy 6:5: "Love the LORD your God with all your heart and with all your soul and with all your strength." Remove all animosity from your heart for those people that have mistreated you, because you have the powerful love of God. You are an extension of God's love on this earth. The world is dying due to the lack of love. Today, commit to cultivating the Fruit of the Spirit-Love.

Today's Declaration:

I am a demonstration of Christ on the earth. As God has commanded, I love all. I am merciful, just as my Father is merciful. Luke 6:36

Love the Lord
Unconditionally

The LORD has put it on my heart to share with you Proverbs 8:17-21. It reads, "I love all who love me. Those who search for me will surely find me. Unending riches, honor, wealth, and justice are mine to distribute. My gifts are better than the purest gold. My wages are better than silver. I walk in righteousness, in paths of injustice. Those who love me inherit wealth, for I fill their treasuries." The LORD formed the beginning before anything else. I hope this fills you as it has me. May your life continue to be flooded by love, peace, and prosperity and may God do more for you than you thought possible.

Today's Declaration:

The LORD blesses me and keeps me. He makes His face to shine on me and be gracious to me. The LORD turns His face towards me and gives me peace. I will follow Him all the days of my life. Numbers 6:24-26

Humility

My Purpose Is Important

I am vital and intelligent, and I listen to life. I am an important human being and my very essence of life is vital. God has a purpose for me, and my purpose is to fulfill my destiny. I am strong-willed and strong-minded and He has created me uniquely for my divine purpose. Exodus 9:16: "But I have raised you up for this very purpose, that I might show you my power and that my name might be proclaimed in all the earth." Look, listen and be mindful of your purpose so that you may fulfill your destiny.

Today's Declaration:

God trusts me with great assignments. He has put His words in my mouth and appointed me over nations and kingdoms to uproot and tear down, to destroy and overthrow, to build and to plant. I have a wonderful assignment within the Kingdom of God. Jeremiah 1:10

It's Not About Us

We are born to make evident the glory of God that is within us. God shines His light through us to reach other people so that we may liberate ourselves as well as other people. 1 Chronicles 16:10: "Glory in his holy name; let the hearts of those who seek the LORD rejoice."

Today's Declaration:

I walk in my Father's ways. I am His duplicate here on earth. I am made perfect by God's love. I dwell in the LORD's presence, His sanctuary. I live on His holy hill. My walk is blameless and I do what is righteous and speak the truth from my heart. Psalm 15:1-2

Let It Be Of God

Just wanted to take a moment to share a scripture with you from Exodus 23:20. It reads, "See, I am sending my angel before you to lead you safely to the land I have prepared for you. Pay attention to him and obey his instructions. If you obey him and follow all my instructions, I will be an enemy to your enemies, and I will oppose those that oppose you." If you don't obey, then imagine what God will hold back from you in your life. God is here for you and always sending His angels to guide us. Sometimes it's hard to follow the soft words we hear, but just think what God would do for us if we did! The conscience that we hear are His angels. Let the angels' voice guide you in your life. Now, listen with a new set of ears to hear the angels that are always by your side.

Today's Declaration:

I declare that my eyes and ears are blessed. Many prophets and kings wanted to see what I see but did not see it; and hear what I hear but did not hear it. I am in constant communication with the Holy Spirit. Luke 10:23-24

Be Wise In The Words You Choose

It is not always what you say but how you say it. Be wise when talking to people. Your words may affect them more than you know. Talk to them as you would talk to God, with compassion. Proverbs 12:18: "Reckless words pierce like a sword, but the tongue of the wise brings healing." Your words have the ability to heal someone's soul or destroy their self-worth. What you're saying or thinking about yourself is important as well. You can 'speak' yourself to a new dimension...or disqualify yourself for your next blessing. Proverbs 15:4 says, "The tongue that brings healing is a tree of life, but a deceitful tongue crushes the spirit." What is your tongue saying today? Speak life.

Today's Declaration:

I speak life. I can call those things, which be not as though they were. The tongue has the power of life and death. Today, I speak life. Proverbs 18:21

I Will Humble Myself As I Restore My Soul

I rest beside the calm and still waters of a river. I am quiet and at peace with the world. I feel rejuvenated. As I relax my body, my mind becomes more at ease. My soul is restored. My spirit is renewed. It was at the very point when all seemed doomed and I was feeling inadequate when the precious, peaceful presence of God restored my soul. "He leads me beside still waters; he restores my soul." Psalm 23:2-3. When life throws obstacles in your way and all seems impossible, it is important for you to stand. Stand your ground and be patient, for the ground you walk on is holy. Let God calm your waters.

Today's Declaration:

I am a beautiful creation. God loves me! The light of God's face shine upon me this day! Psalm 4:6

Even Small Things Are Important

As you set out on today's journey, take a minute, close your eyes and thank God for today's blessings. We are here and breathing because of His love, His power, and most of all, His mercy. God is doing some miraculous things in your life as He has been doing in mine. Sometimes our blessings are smaller than we had hoped for and they are overlooked. Take time to notice the small blessings so you will be able to acknowledge how great your bigger blessing really is. Pray that He continues to bless you this week and fill you with love, hope, peace, and faith. Remember, faith, no matter how small, is HUGE.

Today's Declaration:

God is doing wonderful things in my life! I am thankful for His blessings. I am exceedingly blessed. I give thanks unto the LORD, for He is good. His love for me endures forever.
1Chronicles 16:34

Thank the Lord at All Times

Whenever it seems black with no way out, and you're feeling like you're falling into darkness and there is no end, try God! God knows and sees all. He is just waiting on your request. If you are on the other end of the spectrum and things are going well and you are feeling on top of the word, don't forget to thank Him. We often times forget to thank God when we are doing well. Remember, those blessings came from Him so that you could prosper. Philippians 4:19: "For my God shall supply all your needs...

Today's Declaration:

I am chosen by God. He gives me the treasures of darkness and riches stored in secret places so that I may know He is God. I honor the LORD with my life today. Isaiah 45:3

Bow Before the Lord

Humble yourself before the LORD. Recognize and respect His power. Those who humble themselves and do what other people are not willing to do, will get what other people want. Job 8:7: "Your beginnings will seem humble, so prosperous will your future be."

Today's Declarations:

I acknowledge and honor God for He has surely given this territory (be specific: business deal, position, etc.) into my hands. Joshua 2:24

Treat Others with Respect

Be mindful in everything that you do: how you act towards other people and how they perceive you. Be patient, kind, and respectful to others, as you would want the same in return. Don't ask others to do something that you are not willing to do yourself. You reap what you sow, so why not plant good seeds so that you may reap the benefits cheerfully? "In everything do to others as you would have them do to you; for this is the law and the prophets." Matthew 7:12

Today's Declaration:

I treat others as I want to be treated. This pleases the LORD. I am blessed of God and made in His likeness and image. I am fruitful and multiply. I subdue and have dominion over the earth.
Genesis 1:26

There Is Power Is Prayer

Ephesians 6:18 says, "Praying always with all prayer and supplication in the spirit, and watching there unto with all perseverance and supplication for all saints. Pray in the spirit at all times in all prayers, asking for everything you need." Never give in. Also pray for all of God's people. God has commanded us to pray for others, even our enemies, as we would pray for ourselves. Remain faithful and steadfast and know God will give you what He has promised you.

Today's Declaration:

I seek the LORD in all things. Because I believe that I have received, whatever I ask for in prayer is done for me. I receive the full blessings of the LORD. Mark 11:24

Passion

The Kingdom Is Waiting On You

In 2nd Chronicles 1:11 and 12 God said to Solomon, "Since this is your heart's desire and you have not asked for wealth, riches or honor, nor for the death of your enemies, and since you have not asked for a long life but for wisdom and knowledge to govern my people over whom I have made you king, therefore wisdom and knowledge will be given you.' God will make you king in your own right. If you ask for wisdom, you will lead many people to their destiny. Wisdom is what's needed to get to the next dimension. What are you waiting for?

Today's Declaration:

I approach the throne of God boldly and full of expectation. I ask for wisdom. God gives wisdom generously to all without finding fault. I am not double-minded, for I believe and do not doubt. I have received the wisdom of God! James 1:5-8

All That I Am

I am a believer in Jesus Christ who is the head of my life. All that I am and will ever be is because He has blessed me tremendously. I thank you LORD every day for life, health and strength. You are my rock, redeemer and my salvation. Without you, I am nothing. But with you I am a child of God with everlasting life.

Today's Declaration:

I am the righteousness of God. The LORD blesses the righteous. He surrounds me with favor as with a shield! LORD, I glorify you today with my very life! Psalm 5:12

We Will Serve the Lord

A house divided is a house that is doomed for disaster. Make sure that your house is in order and that God is at the head of your house. Joshua 24:15: "But if serving the LORD seems undesirable to you, then choose for yourselves this day whom you will serve, whether the gods your forefathers served beyond the River, or the gods of the Amorites, in whose land you are living. But as for me and my household, we will serve the LORD." Cast out every demon out of your house and praise the LORD.

Today's Declaration:

I choose this day who I will serve. As for me and my house, we will serve the LORD. Joshua 24:15

Worship the Lord in Praise

Let the teaching of Christ live richly in you. Use all wisdom to teach and instruct each other by singing psalms, hymns, and spiritual songs with thankfulness in your hearts to God. Everything you do or say should be done to obey Jesus your LORD. And in all you do, give thanks to God the Father through Jesus. Colossians 3:16-17

Today's Declaration

I worship God with all that I am. I give thanks to the LORD because of His righteousness and sing praise to His name. My heart is filled with His love and praises! Psalm 7:17

I Have a Deep Desire To Connect With the Lord

Devoting time to meditation, prayer, and contemplation, I make choices from an inner place of wisdom and peace. These are spiritual experiences that help me obtain a deep awareness of God that cannot be undone by any outer condition. In conscious communion with God, I understand my relationship with God and my relationships with the people in my life. "Talk no more so very proudly, for the LORD is a God of knowledge, and by him actions are weighed." --1 Samuel 2:3 Take the time you need to understand that God is working miracles in your life right now, even though you may not see them right away. He may not come when you want Him but He is always on time.

Today's Declaration:

God is my provider. Therefore, I do not live on bread alone, but on every word that comes from the mouth of the LORD. Deuteronomy 8:3

Believe In Your Path

Your loved ones should always be in your thoughts and prayers. As I go to God, I am led to tell you that the strength and courage you need lies within, but you have to believe in it. God said, 'I am the truth and the light. Today, I give you light, wish you peace and charge you to believe in your strength. You can surely do all things through Christ Jesus, who strengthens you. Step out on faith and do what you know you can. Take it a step further...step out into the deep. Do something you've failed at previously. Test the strength of God within you. Allow Him to blow your mind and knock you off your feet. May God be with you on your journey. I declare that your trials are blessed and that there is instant healing for family members that are sick and down. Be strong in the LORD!

Today's Declaration:

I am strong and very courageous. I do not walk in fear. I am careful to obey God's laws. Therefore, I am successful wherever I go.
Joshua 1:7

Nothing Can Break Bond With My Lord and Savior

God is my provider, protector and my defense. His presence surrounds and enfolds me to an unbreakable level. While the devil may be busy, consistently trying to destroy me, God is on the clock watching over me and shielding my soul. Deuteronomy 23:14: "For the LORD your God moves about in your camp to protect you and to deliver your enemies to you." Your camp must be holy, so that he will not see among you anything indecent and turn away from you.

Today's Declaration:

God is the first and the last. Apart from Him there is no God. I have no idols. I worship God only- not my job, my spouse, my position or my children. God is the One and Only. Isaiah 44:6

I Want To Be Edified
by God's Word

LORD, let the words of my mouth and the meditation of my heart be acceptable in your sight, allow me to read and study your word on a daily basis. Joshua 1:8: "Do not let this Book of the Law depart from your mouth; meditate on it day and night, so that you may be careful to do everything written in it. Then you will be prosperous and successful." Let me heed your words so that I may teach others about the kingdom and all its glory.

Today's Declaration:

I grow daily in the Word. I study to show myself approved, having full understanding of the Word of God. 2 Timothy 2:15

Live Your Life According To God

I thank you LORD for being an awesome friend, one who gives so much. Deuteronomy 8:1: "Be careful to follow every command I am giving you today, so that you may live and increase and may enter and possess the land that the LORD promised on oath to your forefathers." You will have increase in your life because you are faithful and you give of yourself so much. Don't worry about what you are receiving as much as what you are giving to others.

Today's Declaration:

I am prosperous and successful. I do not let the Word depart from my mouth. I meditate on the Word day and night so that I am careful to do everything in it. Joshua 1:8

Forgiveness

Remove All Negativity

Oh, what a blessed day! Let this be the week that you make choices to change your life. May God bless you and strengthen you in this time of worship and praise. May He help you to prosper more than you thought possible, heal you and bless your family situations. May peace be restored; your cloud of negativity be gone. May He give you guidance where you feel you're traveling blind. May He answer that one prayer that you have been praying for quite some time. May He touch your heart that you may forgive those that wronged you as He forgave you for all the wrong you have done. May God have mercy on your heart, my heart, and the heart of the world. May He love you and keep you eternally safe.

Today's Declaration:

I walk in love towards those who love me and those who hate me. I love my enemies and do good to those who hate me, bless those who curse me and pray for those who mistreat me. Luke 6:27-28

You Have a Second Chance

Don't worry about the troubles you had in the past, your sometimes 'wicked ways'. All you have to do is get down on your knees and pray for forgiveness, because the person who you are today is different from the person you were yesterday. Psalm 25:7: "Remember not the sins of my youth, nor my transgressions: according to thy mercy remember thou me for thy goodness' sake, O LORD." The LORD sees you for who you are today!

Today's Declaration:

I worship God with all that I am. I confess my sins and God forgives me. I give thanks to the LORD because of His righteousness and sing praises to His name. Psalm 7:17

Ask God for Help

Days are passing and storms are raging, but the best is yet to come! I pray that God fills you with just what you need to survive in your situation. People are quick to comment and try to tell you how you should handle things. But today, close your ears to people and open your mouth to God. You and only God know your situation, and you and God are going to bring you through. You are going to bring greatness out of a great mess. Greatness is what He wants to bestow upon you. Be blessed and know that no matter what, you have already survived your situation. Rejoice, even during the raging storm! Praise your way out!

Today's Declaration:

I am one of God's favorite. I praise the LORD who councils me, even at night my heart instructs me. I will not worry about issues in my life. Psalm 16:7

Even the Righteous Falls

As you accept Christ and believe in Him, He will guide, protect and lead you to the path of righteousness. He will forgive you of all your sins. If a just man falls seven times and is forgiven, surely you will be forgiven also. Acts 10:43: "All the prophets testify about him that everyone who believes in him receives forgiveness of sins through his name."

Today's Declaration:

LORD, thank you for your amazing grace! I won't go through life looking back. I am guided in the way of wisdom and led along straight paths. When I walk my steps are not hampered. Great things are in store for me! Proverbs 4:12

I Strive To Be Christ Like

I love the LORD with all my heart.   Therefore, I love my neighbor as well. Leviticus 19:18: "Do not seek revenge or bear a grudge against one of your people, but love your neighbor as yourself. I am the LORD."   In order for you to be Christ-like you have to have the ability to love all people because they are all children of God. You may not like the things that they do but love them nonetheless. You are an example of Christ on this earth.

Today's Declaration:

I am a demonstration of Christ on the earth.   As God has commanded, I love all.   I am merciful, just as my Father is merciful. Luke 6:3

Do Not Harden Your Heart

Through the Spirit of Christ within me, I forgive others and myself. The LORD revealed in 2 Chronicles 7:14: "If my people, who are called by my name, will humble themselves and pray and seek my face and turn from their wicked ways, then will I hear from heaven and will forgive their sins and will heal their land." The LORD will heal your body; He will heal your money; and He will heal your broken heart if you humble yourself and pray. Repent for all the wrong deeds, thoughts and actions. Surrender yourself to Him. It is at this point that He will hear, forgive and heal you.

Today's Declaration:

I will walk in a surrendered posture towards God. I seek God with all my heart today. The light of God's face shines on me, for He has filled my heart with greater joy. Psalm 4:6-7

A Merciful God

The LORD is ever kind and ever merciful even when we don't deserve it. He has blessed us even when we did not deserve a blessing. But His mercy endures and His love is everlasting.
2 Samuel 2:6: "May the LORD now show you kindness and faithfulness, and I too will show you the same favor because you have done this." May the favor of the LORD be upon your heart.

Today's Declaration:

Thank you, LORD, for blessing me! My soul delights in the LORD. I trust in His unfailing love. My heart rejoices in His salvation. I sing to the LORD because He has been good to me.
Psalm 13:5-6

Don't Fight God's Battles

Many times people have mistreated you, talked about you and stabbed you in the back. It is not for you to take revenge against them. Let the battle be the LORD's. Leviticus 19:18: "Do not seek revenge or bear a grudge against one of your people, but love your neighbor as yourself. I am the LORD." He can handle any situation better than we can, so let God do His work.

Today's Declaration:

I will not ponder the negative circumstances. I will walk in peace. For this battle is not mine, but God's. 2 Chronicles 20:15

Faith

God Will Never Leave You

Before you go into any situation, say a powerful prayer and ask the LORD to go before you to handle the circumstance. Allow the LORD to work His wonders before you put your hands on it because His hands are mighty.

Deuteronomy 31:8: "The LORD himself goes before you and will be with you; he will never leave you nor forsake you. Do not be afraid; do not be discouraged." You need not to fear nor worry when God is in control.

Today's Declaration:

I am strong and mighty. I am the head and not the tail; above only and never beneath because I keep the commands of the LORD and follow them carefully. Deuteronomy 28:13

Believe What God Has For You

Your destiny is right before your feet. Acknowledge God and He will reveal it to you.

Deuteronomy 30:5: "He will bring you to the land that belonged to your fathers, and you will take possession of it. He will make you more prosperous and numerous than your fathers." Then take back what is rightfully yours and claim your victory. Once you understand who you are in Christ, hell won't be able to keep you from your destiny!

Today's Declaration:

Victory is mine! I honor God Almighty. I live in increase and God has blessed me in the land I'm possessing because I walk in His ways and keep His commands. Deuteronomy 30:16

I Am In the Will of God

The Will of God never takes you to where the Grace of God will not protect you. Job 22:21: "Submit to God and be at peace with him; in this way prosperity will come to you." Allow the Grace of God to overtake you and keep you.

Today's Declaration:

Thank God for His amazing grace! Because He loves me, He keeps me and protects me. Because I love Him, I declare that it is in Him that I live, move and have my very being! I am His offspring! Acts 17:28

My Faith Is Everlasting

The LORD wants your conviction to be strong. He wants your foundation to be powerful, and your faith to be everlasting. You are to be deeply rooted in the word, in the Spirit, and in the presence and the knowledge of God. Psalm 1:3: "He is like a tree planted by streams of water, which yields its fruit in season and whose leaf does not wither. Whatever he does prospers."

Today's Declaration:

I will God's Word in my heart and on my lips. I have a teachable spirit and operate as an apostle, prophet, evangelist, pastor and teacher to prepare God's people for works of service so that the body of Christ may be built up. Ephesians 4:11-12

Believe the Wonders of God

There are times when you need to pray for someone other than yourself. Prayer is a powerful thing that has the ability to change circumstances, people, and the world. When the prayers go up the blessings come down. Job 42:10: "After Job had prayed for his friends, the LORD made him prosperous again and gave him twice as much as he had before."

Today's Declaration:

I am constantly communicating with God. He hears my prayers and answers them. I rejoice always; pray without ceasing.
1 Thessalonians 5:16-17

Taking the First Step

It is your job to plant seeds and water them along the way. God will provide the sunshine to help them become fruitful. You will never prosper without first planting your seeds. I never knew a farmer who reaped a plentiful harvest without first planting his seeds. Genesis 26:12: "Isaac planted crops in that land and the same year reaped a hundredfold, because the LORD blessed him." You do your part and allow the LORD to do His. The LORD helps those who help themselves.

Today's Declaration:

I plant good seeds into good soil. As I have done, it will be done to me; my deeds will return. I sow good seeds to further establish the kingdom of God. Obadiah 1:5

Make My Dream a Reality

If you are a dreamer and never an achiever you will never have anything but dreams. If you are a person that watches things happen and never makes things happen, you will never accomplish anything. Ecclesiastes 11:4: "Whoever watches the wind will not plant; whoever looks at the clouds will not reap." In order for you to get what you want you must step out on faith and make things happen.

Today's Declaration:

I am a servant of the Most High God. I am a dreamer and an achiever. I do not forget the word that I have heard. I perform the word I've heard. Therefore, I am blessed in what I do. James 1:25

Nothing Is Impossible

Today is the day I decide to stand and make changes in my life that will change the rest of my life. I will fear no evil and obey the LORD, as He is my Prince of Peace and my salvation. Joshua 1:7: "Be strong and very courageous. Be careful to obey all the law my servant Moses gave you; do not turn from it to the right or to the left, that you may be successful wherever you go."

Today's Declaration:

I have no limitations. Nothing is impossible to achieve because nothing is too hard for God. Genesis 18:14

I Hear You Lord

Do not be fooled by those who think they know everything. A person who thinks they know everything is often a fool because they think they can learn nothing. Listen to your inner self and hear God's words and see His vision for your life. Deuteronomy 13:3: "You must not listen to the words of that prophet or dreamer. The LORD your God is testing you to find out whether you love him with all your heart and with all your soul."

Today's Declaration:

I will not be deterred today! I am a mighty child of God. His commands make me wiser than my enemies. I have more insight than all my teachers because I meditate on His statues. I have more understanding than the elders because I obey God's precepts. Psalm 119:99-100

God Is On the Job

Stop trying to do God's work! Let God be God, and you do the job that you are supposed to do. When you get in God's business you are touching something that is already handled. You keep fighting a battle that is already won by God. So just be still and stand and let God fight for you. 2 Chronicles 20:15: "This is what the LORD says to you: do not be afraid or discouraged because of this vast army. For the battle is not yours, but God's."

Today's Declaration:

I do what is right and good in the LORD's sight, so I may go in and take over the good land God promised me. He thrusts out all my enemies before me. There's no one like the LORD!
Deuteronomy 6:18-19

Prayer

Almighty Father,

I ask you to bless my friends, relatives and those that I care deeply for. Show them a new revelation of your love and power. Holy Spirit, I ask you to minister to their spirit at this very moment. Where there is pain, give them your peace and mercy. Where there is self-doubt, release a renewed confidence through your grace. Where there is need, I ask you to fulfill their needs. Bless their homes, families, finances, their goings and their comings. In Jesus' precious name I pray. Amen

Today's Declaration:

I am a disciple of the Most High. As commanded, I go into all the world and preach the good news to all creation. I am all that God created me to be.
Mark 16:15

Dear LORD and Savior,

I pray that you will bless and uplift my friends. I want my friends to experience riches and joy, peace and sanity, hope and love. If my friends have done any wrong, please forgive them. LORD, open the eyes of their hearts so they may see and repent. I pray that you will help them to have a wonderful week free of the daily stressor and stress factors, which sometimes come in the form of people. I pray that you continue to love them and grant that one wish that they so desire. I love you God. I pray that you be their light and their conscious when they need you most. Amen

Today's Declaration:

I trust in the LORD and His word. His word will not return to Him void, but will accomplish that which He spoke. He is not a man that He should lie nor the son of man that He should change His mind. Numbers 23:19

Dear GOD,

I want to thank you for what you have already done. I am not going to wait until I see results or receive rewards; I am thanking you right now. I am not going to wait until I feel better or things look better; I am thanking you right now. I am not going to wait until people say they are sorry or until they stop talking about me; I am thanking you right now. I am not going to wait until the pain in my body disappears; I am thanking you right now. I am not going to wait until my financial situation improves; I am going to thank you right now. I am not going to wait until the children are asleep and the house is quiet; I am going to thank you right now. I am not going to wait until I get promoted at work or until I get the job; I am going to thank you right now. I am not going to wait until I understand every experience in my life that has caused me pain or grief; I am thanking you right now. I am not going to wait until the journey gets easier or the challenges are removed; I am thanking you right now. I am thanking you because I am alive. I am thanking you because I made it through the day's difficulties. I am thanking you because I have walked around the obstacles. I am thanking you because I have the ability and the opportunity to do more and do better. I'm thanking you because FATHER, YOU haven't given up on me.

Today's Declaration

God is the first and the last. Apart from Him there is no God. I have no idols. I worship God only- not my job, my spouse, my position or my children. God is the One and Only. Isaiah 44:6

About the Author

Dr. Donavan Outten is a powerful and energetic motivational speaker, entrepreneur and President of Educate U Foundation, an organization dedicated to helping to decrease the Achievement Gap in America. Dr. Outten is so dedicated to the cause of youth development that all proceeds from the sales of this book will go to research, training, program development and scholarships for minorities and underrepresented youth.

Dr. Outten has dedicated the last 20 years of his life to education. Most recently he has held administrator positions at Upper Iowa University and Unity College. Both domestically and internationally he gives inspirational lectures and keynote addresses at conferences, universities, churches,

and community organizations. Dr.
Outten is also the author of Skills for
Success, a book dedicated to imparting
the skills for living a life of success. Dr.
Outten is led and moved by the spirit of
God, and it shows through his work.

Made in the USA
San Bernardino, CA
30 May 2014